Love from Mum
xxxx

Life's Little Delights

MEGAN HESS

First published in 2003 by
Judy Piatkus (Publishers) Limited
5 Windmill Street
London W1T 2JA

Website: www.piatkus.co.uk
Email: info@piatkus.co.uk

The moral right of the author has
been asserted. A catalogue record for
this book is available from the
British Library.

ISBN 0 7499 2466 7

Text design and setting by
Mark Latter at Vivid

This book has been printed on paper
manufactured with respect for the
environment using wood from managed
sustainable resources

Printed in China for Imago

For Neville Hume, my grandad,
who saw every single day as a delight.

Acknowledgements

**To everyone below who in some
way has helped me create this book...**

Alice Davis, for moving mountains
to make this book happen and for fulfilling
a lifelong dream of mine.

Judy Piatkus, for a great brainstorming session
over muffins and coffee in Melbourne.

My husband Craig, for helping me with every single
page of this book (architects are very good with
perspective) and making me believe I can do anything.

My Mum, for driving me to art lessons every
Saturday as a kid and making me the person I am today.

My Dad, for Sunday omelettes
and always believing in me.

My sister Kerrie, for being my partner
in crime. You've been my best friend
since we could both walk.

To my brother Tom for letting me win
that LEGO competition. It inspired me
to be creative from that day forward!

And finally to my Nan Gwyn, for making me laugh
and giving me the will to never give up.

Finding the perfect pair of shoes

Soaking in the tub
with scented candles

Eating chocolate

Hearing from an old friend

Leaving work to go on holiday

*Treating yourself
to a bunch of flowers*

*Hearing your favourite
song on the radio*

Standing under a hot shower

Lying in bed
listening to the rain

Getting pampered

Finding the perfect object for your home

Sale

Dancing all night

Making a new friend

Laughing so hard
your stomach hurts

Finding the outfit you
really want is in the sale

Walking barefoot
by the edge of the sea

Watching your favourite film
... again

Getting ready for
a big night out

*Having lunch with
your best friend*

Making eye contact with an attractive stranger

*Kicking your shoes off
after a night out*

Giving the perfect gift

Being first at a newly opened checkout

Eating cake

*Sitting down after
a day's shopping*

Finding money in your pocket

Waking up and realizing
you don't have to get up yet

Throwing a fabulous party

Watching the sun set